CHRISTIAN GRATITUDE JOURNAL

Name:

Email:

Phone:

7 STEPS TO

LIFE-CHANGING APPRECIATION

by Mike Jones

Christian Gratitude Journal, 7 Steps to Life-Changing Appreciation

First Edition 3rd Revision. 2022.02ii
Published February 2021. Revised February 2022.
Copyright © 2021 Mike Jones

All rights reserved. No part of this publication may be reproduced, distributed, or transmitted in any form or by any means, including photocopying, recording, or other electronic or mechanical methods, without the prior written permission of the publisher, except in the case of brief quotations embodied in critical reviews and certain other non-commercial uses permitted by copyright law. For permission requests, write to the publisher at the address below.

Joyskills Press. 32 Whitehill Ave, Luton, LU1 3SP

joyskillsjoy@gmail.com

www.joyskills.online

Joyskills® is registered Trademark in the United Kingdom

AMP Scripture quotations marked (AMP) are taken from the Amplified Bible, Copyright © 1954, 1958, 1962, 1964, 1965, 1987 by The Lockman Foundation. Used by permission.

ESV: Scripture quotations are from The Holy Bible, English Standard Version ® (ESV ®), copyright © 2001 by Crossway, a publishing ministry of Good News Publishers. Used by permission. All rights reserved

KJV: The Holy Bible: King James Version. (2009). Electronic Edition of the 1900 Authorized Version. . Bellingham, WA: Logos Research Systems, Inc.

MSG: "Scripture taken from The Message. Copyright © 1993, 1994, 1995, 1996, 2000, 2001, 2002. Used by permission of NavPress Publishing Group."

NCV: Scripture taken from the New Century Version ®. Copyright © 2005 by Thomas Nelson. Used by permission. All rights reserved.

NKJV: Scripture taken from the New King James Version ®. Copyright © 1982 by Thomas Nelson. Used by permission. All rights reserved.

Scripture quotations marked (NIV) are taken from the Holy Bible, New International Version, NIV ®. Copyright © 1973, 1978, 1984, 2011 by Biblica, Inc.® Used by permission of Zondervan. All rights reserved worldwide. www.zondervan.com The "NIV" and "New International Version" are trademarks registered in the United States Patent and Trademark Office by Biblica, Inc.®

ACKNOWLEDGMENTS

For Ruth my love and companion;
For mum and dad for your constant love;
For everyone at St Mary's our friends and co-travelers in these difficult days;
For Bill and Susan; Ben and Chris for your love and support;
For Verulam House Trust Fund and Ecclesiastical Insurance who enabled us to go to Thrive;
For Jim Wilder, Andrew Miller and Karl Lehman for the depth of your insight;
For the transforming friendship of walking with God;
I will always be grateful and thankful.

CONTENTS

Contents	5
Introduction	7
What are the benefits for me?	8
Why this journal?	8
I'm Inconsistent. What should I do?	9
Can you explain the layout?	10
Step 1 Start!	12
Step 2 Remember good things	16
Step 3 Relive positive memories	20
Step 4 Engage with your God-memories	26
Step 5 Do it through the day	36
Step 6 Intentional gratitude	42
Step 7 Changing your world	54
Congratulations	70
References	78
Notes & Ideas	78
Appreciation Memories List	84
Appreciation Cycle	86
Index	87

GIVE THANKS TO THE LORD FOR HE IS GOOD. HIS LOVE ENDURES FOREVER

PSALM 136:1

INTRODUCTION

"This is a fabulous book that helps you look at the good things in your life. It helped to lift me out of depression." Amazon Review.

We all want to flourish. Yet, if we look around us, people are struggling. Few have learned the secret to flourishing consistently and predictably.

Resources that can help exist, but they are locked away inside the Bible and inside the minds of Christian psychologists and psychiatrists. Although most of us are unaware of them, there are ways to thrive amid difficulties. This book shows you how.

It's a well-known key that's usually misunderstood. Thankfulness opens the door to a happier life - but this is not any old gratitude. A typical gratitude practice comprises a few steps. Initially, they tell you to remember things and then instruct you to do so throughout the day. However, there are additional steps to take. There are other steps in this journal, which are based on over 60 years of Christian ministry experience.

Clinical psychologist Dr Jim Wilder and psychiatrist Karl Lehman have each devoted 30 years to the overlap between our walk with Jesus, thanksgiving and thriving. This is the first gratitude journal based on their work. During my research into their life-changing ministries, they changed my life and can do the same for you. Using this tool can lead to more joy, more peace, and an improved walk with Jesus. You will improve your whole life and your relationships by doing this.

Marriages, businesses, churches are flourishing using the insights in this book. Dr Lehman helps married couples, Dr Warner helps businesses, Michael Hendricks consults with churches all using the insights from the Life Model revealed in this journal.

When faced with work stress, family illness, and forced move due to water damage, I resolved not just to survive but to thrive. As I embarked on a journey of daily gratitude, I experienced a warmth and a lightness in my chest that replaced the tightness caused by stress. By being happier, I could help my family, church, and others. You can experience these benefits, too.

Isn't this what you want as a Christian? To thrive rather than merely survive? Read this book, do the exercises and find out for yourself that "we enter his gates with thanksgiving."

WHAT ARE THE BENEFITS FOR ME?

This journal will help you
- improve your mood;
- improve your relationships
- get promoted
- experience God's presence;
- become more like Jesus.

Use the journal
- in your quiet time;
- in your family;
- in your small group;
- in your church.
- in your workplace;

WHY *THIS* JOURNAL?

The journal

- **Works because it is based in practice.** I have used it for myself and in groups. This means that it contains practical exercises which work. It takes time and a series of steps to grow in appreciation and the journal is based around those.
- **Contains stories.** Because I published the book on Amazon, I have updated it with stories that bring to life the points being made.
- **Has a biblical basis.** Thanksgiving is a foundational Christian habit and perspective. As 1 Thessalonians 5:16-18 puts it, "Rejoice always, pray continually, give thanks in all circumstances; for this is God's will for you in Christ Jesus." It has Bible verses throughout the pages.
- **Is designed to help you grow in your relationships - with God and others.**
- **Works because it takes seriously the way God made our brains.** Brain science has showed us why the biblical call to be thankful is so

smart. It also helps us see why lengthening the time we spend in thankfulness and improving the way we do it helps us pray, relate to others and feel better.

- **Is a helpful resource.** You can use the exercises with your family, with children, in Bible studies or in your services if you are a pastor. Last week, a pastor messaged me to say how it had brought blessing to a married couple he was working with while other people use the exercises to start their small group. I summarize its teaching in an **Appreciation Cycle** that you can use for yourself, in a small group or when leading a service.

I'M INCONSISTENT. WHAT SHOULD I DO?

KEEP THE JOURNAL IN PLAIN SIGHT

My recommendation is that you have the journal "in plain sight". The phrase "out of sight, out of mind," is true. Put the journal where you might use it with a pen / pencil nearby. I bring it with me in my bag and use it in spare moments or when I want a boost.

ASK YOURSELF, "WHAT IS MY GOAL FOR INVESTING MY TIME IN THIS JOURNAL?"

As you start this journey, it makes a massive difference if you decide what your aims are.

JUST DO IT

Read the first pages and do the first exercise now!

Just do it! Start! That's Step 1.

CAN YOU EXPLAIN THE LAYOUT?

The journal has seven steps plus a "Continuing the Journey" section.

The steps take you on a journey of growth.

There are topical pages such as "Pets I am Grateful for."

There are also Daily 1-2-3 pages which have
- Letters to circle which abbreviate the day of the week from Monday to Sunday: M T W T F S S.
- A space for a date.
- A Bible verse.

All you do is circle the day, write the date, read the Bible verse, and write three things you appreciate. If you are in a hurry, you can do this quickly and move on. Alternatively, you can use them in a more leisurely and reflective way.

At the back of the journal is an Appreciation Cycle which summarizes the book, a topical index, and space for you to index your journal entries.

THE FIRST STEPS TO FEELING GREAT!

STEP 1 START!

My mum taught me to say, "thank you." to people and send thank you notes for gifts. Appreciation begins there and actively extends it outwards wider and wider.

Appreciation is the "recognition and enjoyment of the good qualities of someone or something," (Oxford Dictionary). We begin our journey with recognizing good qualities in something or someone.

We begin by noticing the value of something and naming it - to yourself or to other people. To start appreciation, you focus your attention on it and notice the good about it.

As you do this, things may start to change. If I wake up in the morning, taking time to appreciate the positives of those I will meet or the people in my life changes my mood, helps me find the good in the day ahead, and helps me pray for God to be at work. This can be true for you too.

Whenever I lead people in times of appreciation, often particular places or scenes come to mind. A specific beach, house, town, mountain or room might appear in someone's mind; or they may picture a lake, hill, forest or a seaside. Memory works this way.

As a kid my biggest problem with thank you notes was starting. I would never get round to it. Three weeks after Christmas my mum would force me to write my thank yous! So Step 1 is Start!

As you read this , think of a place that is positive for you

- Bring the place to life in your mind.
- Think of specific events that happened there.
- Note them down on the next page.

DON'T WORRY IF IT IS DIFFICULT

My friend Chris Coursey now writes about the power of appreciation. Yet, when he first practiced appreciation he struggled. See what he says in his book, The 4 Habits of Joy-Filled Marriages,

When I first started being intentional about building the habit of appreciation, I struggled with anxiety. I discovered that anxiety can make it pretty hard to stay in appreciation mode. The first time I intentionally decided to spend five minutes in a state of appreciation, my experience went something like this. I grabbed my favorite coffee mug and prepared my favorite blend of cream, sugar, and coffee, then held the mug in my hands and breathed in the aroma. I had just started to enjoy the moment

Jesus modeled appreciation in his life. As he feeds the 5000 he thanks God before generously sharing out the food in this miraculous provision.

when my left brain chimed in and said, "This is the stupidest thing you've ever done!"

Instead of helping me quiet my anxious thoughts, I became more agitated. I am so left-brain dominant that my ability to actually appreciate what I was experiencing was easily sabotaged. Because I hadn't been practicing appreciation as a normal part of my life, it was nearly impossible to flip the switch and engage my right brain just by choice. I learned that it can take weeks of intentional practice to build joy through a routine of focused appreciation (page 91).

Take your time and be gentle with yourself. Remember that Chris who writes on appreciation struggled when he started. The easiest place to start is with people, pets or places. Try the next exercise and see how it goes.

PLACES I APPRECIATE ARE...

Whenever I lead people in times of appreciation and they share examples, often they will involve people, pets or places. Today, think of some places you appreciate.

- Write them in the space below.
- What are the good things about them?
- Spend some time giving thanks for specific memories that come to mind, then put them on the list below.
- Give each memory a short title that summarizes it.

When Jacob woke up, he thought, "Surely the LORD is in this place, and I was unaware of it." And he was afraid and said, "How awesome is this place! This is none other than the house of God; this is the gate of heaven!"... and he called that place Bethel. Genesis 28:16-19 (NIV).

ENJOYING IT

As we said, Appreciation is the "recognition and enjoyment of the good qualities of someone or something," (Oxford Dictionary). Often the gratitude journey begins in recognition of the good, then we turn to enjoyment.

For example, thanking my wife for cooking dinner is one thing. Enjoying her brilliance as a cook and spending time in appreciation of it until I feel grateful is another thing entirely. When I sit in thankfulness for long enough and feel it, thinking turns to feeling which changes our relationship.

Let's call that feeling gratitude. Let's think of it as a feeling or a state of thankfulness. It's about what you feel or sense rather than what you think.

- For some it's more a feeling;
- For others it's a mood state or sensation;
- Many people feel very little gratitude at all.

Taking time to dwell on what I appreciate about my son Chris changes how I feel about him. Taking time to dwell on the positives of my job change how I feel about it when I fell overworked and under appreciated. Thinking about my daughter Alex while she lived overseas, kept my feelings for her alive.

Time in thankfulness creates feelings which change how we live our lives. Feelings impact people's day-to-day experience more than they realize. For example, when I am overwhelmed, I create a strained atmosphere around me. When I notice what is happening, I will grab this journal and spend 5-25 minutes in recognizing the good about things and prayer until I feel gratitude rising above overwhelm.

A couple of months ago, I spent two hours doing this when life was tense. I emerged from that "quiet time" in a happier and more constructive frame of mind that more than made up for the two hours spend in appreciation.

Try the exercise on the next page.

Bless the LORD, O my soul; And all that is within me, bless His holy name! Bless the LORD, O my soul, And forget not all His benefits. Psalm 103:1–2 (NKJV).

WHAT DO I FEEL GRATEFUL FOR?
Consider what you feel grateful for.

Now consider what you feel grateful for. If you can't think of anything, begin with recognizing the good about things. What are the benefits they bring you? The positives they give your life?

Think about pets, a person, a place you like, or an experience you are thankful for. Some people begin by cradling a cup of coffee in their hands and being grateful for that and a moment of calm.

If you feel very little gratitude, that's okay for now. Simply note what you do feel / sense & write the date. If you progress in this area, being honest helps you to track your progress.

Usually, as people do more appreciation exercises and do them for longer, they begin to feel gratitude.

For example, I have two minutes now before going to lunch. I have chosen to think about my wife Ruth. I can feel thankful that she made me a cup of coffee earlier but that doesn't go deep. So I turn my mind to times when she has cared for me when I am ill, or how she looks out for our children when I am busy. I can feel a smile rising on my lips and as I go to lunch I am feeling grateful...

STEP 2 REMEMBER GOOD THINGS

Remembering good things helps us emotionally and enriches our relationships; it can strengthen our faith and help us live in joy and peace.

We can remember people, places, pets and everyday experiences. We can also remember our God-moments and the benefits of our faith. The Bible calls us to remember and appreciate his love for us.

Step 2 is to remember good things and actively recall them. Turn them over in your mind and bring them to life in your imagination.

Think about someone you appreciate and do the next exercise.

SOMEONE I APPRECIATE...

Think about people around you.

What do you value about them?

- What is good and distinctive about them?
- Make notes.
- Recall specific experiences you are grateful for. Remember things they have done for you.
- Now focus on a memorable experience. Take a few moments to recall positive things that come to mind.
- Finally, thank God and pray for anyone who has come to mind.

Then take care lest you forget the Lord, who brought you out of the land of Egypt, out of the house of slaves. Deuteronomy 6:12 (ESV).

USING THE DAILY 1-2-3 PAGES

Many of the right-hand pages are labeled:
- with a day M T W T F S S and
- a space for a date.

I call them Daily 1-2-3 pages. I show the layout below.

The benefit to these pages is that you can complete them in a hurry. Read the Bible verse, write your answers, and then move on. As you go, think about what you have written.

Alternately, you can use them in a more leisurely and reflective manner.

I repeat them because they build a habit of simple gratitude and looking for things we appreciate.

When you complete the Daily 1-2-3 pages:
- Circle the day of the week (the letters stand for Monday, Tuesday, Wednesday, etc.)
- Write the date.
- Complete the activity.

Today's activity is to list three things you appreciate. Big or small, it doesn't matter. I would like you to consider who or what you appreciate and why.

You can complete a sentence like "I appreciate Jack because he is there for my sister;" or it can be about God, "I appreciate God because he is my rock."

You can also think about what makes someone or something unique and special. Thank God and pray for someone at the end of the activity.

M T W T F S S   DATE: _____

Today I appreciate

1

2

3

Dear God thank you....

PETS I AM GRATEFUL FOR...

Today, think of some pets you feel grateful for.

Do you have pleasant experiences and memories of animals? What are you thankful for? Notice where you feel grateful or your body relaxes as you think about your pets.

Spend some time giving thanks for any memories that come to mind, then put them on the list below. Write the name of the animal / kind of animal and two words to summarize a memory you have of them.

If you don't have happy pet memories, then skip this page and complete the Daily 1-2-3 page.

For example, I've been up since 5am and I am sitting in Heathrow Airport Terminal. I'm tired and I want to keep in a good mood. I choose to think of Joby, my daughter's dog. I bring to mind the last time I walked in the door and he ran around the house for joy. I begin smiling as I recall the memory.

Finally, brothers and sisters, whatever is true, whatever is noble, whatever is right, whatever is pure, whatever is lovely, whatever is admirable – if anything is excellent or praiseworthy – think about such things. Philippians 4:8 (NIV).

M T W T F S S   **DATE:** _____

Today I'm grateful for / I give thanks for

1

2

3

Dear God, thank you…

I pray for…

He [Jesus] directed the people to sit down on the grass. Taking the five loaves and the two fish and looking up to heaven, he gave thanks and broke the loaves. Matthew 14:19 (NIV).

M T W T F S S   **DATE:** _____

Today I'm grateful for / I give thanks for

1

2

3

Dear God, thank you…

I pray for…

STEP 3 RELIVE POSITIVE MEMORIES

Reliving positive memories is powerful.

I used to be in a group that began each week with 15 minutes of appreciation. Every Tuesday night, I felt busy, stressed, and anxious. During my time of appreciation, my breathing slowed, I felt less stressed, and my mind became more restful and joyful. I gradually began to feel grateful.

By bringing to life specific memories of someone or something, we engaged the part of our brain that God gave us for daydreaming.

When I used this ability to relive positive memories, I moved from giving thanks (thinking) to gratitude (feeling). I became more grateful as we continued, my body sensations became more peaceful, and I entered a more restful and joyful state of mind.

It wasn't just me. As we spent 15 minutes sharing past experiences that brought gratitude to life, the group's atmosphere warmed up and changed. There was a greater sense of connection in the room. Our relationship became stronger as we felt gratitude together.

This story illustrates the powerful effect of gratitude.

The fuel of giving thanks and gratitude gently warms our brains. The more time we spend in giving thanks and gratitude, the more our mood improves and our brain becomes more friendly and connected.

Spending time in giving thanks and gratitude is worth it. You will reap the rewards. By evoking happy memories in your mind and savoring them, you naturally improve your mood and relationships.

But we must also understand the memories we should avoid.

A bright cloud overshadowed them, and a voice from the cloud said, "This is my dearly loved Son, who brings me great joy. Listen to him." Matthew 17:5b (NLT).

MEMORIES TO AVOID

Try to bring positive memories to life. If a memory arises that has negative associations for you, move on. Choose an alternative memory.

Avoid memories that:
- have the potential to trigger mixed emotions, e.g. tenderness and sadness;
- remind you of people who are no longer around.

Also avoid memories that, though happy,
- would draw you back to addictive or dangerous activities in your life or,
- trigger a sexual response.

You may feel some despair if this means you need to avoid most of your memories. I understand your sadness as this happened to someone close to me. Try memories of current pets, a beautiful walk, a delicious coffee or food, or an experience of God. Unlike your other memories, these are likely to evoke senses and emotions that are safer.

LOOKING BACK: YOUR FAVORITE TOYS AS A CHILD

Imagine your favorite toys as a child. As you remember them, recall some pleasant memories.

If all your childhood memories have sad parts, then try thinking of some recent activities or hobbies that you enjoyed and consider the good memories that accompany them.

I know a couple who loved doing this activity together. Despite 50 years of marriage, when they did this exercise together they discovered new things about each other.

Write some of your memories here:

_____
_____
_____
_____
_____
_____
_____
_____
_____
_____
_____
_____
_____
_____
_____
_____
_____
_____
_____

Every good and perfect gift is from above, coming down from the Father of the heavenly lights. James 1:17 (NIV).

M T W T F S S   **DATE:** _____

I spent time giving thanks / gratitude : __ morning __lunch/afternoon __evening
Today I'm grateful for / I give thanks for
1

2

3

Dear God, thank you…

Is there anything you want to show me?

I pray for…

Praise be to the God and Father of our Lord Jesus Christ, who has blessed us in the heavenly realms with every spiritual blessing in Christ. Ephesians 1:3 (NIV).

M T W T F S S   **DATE:** _____

I spent time giving thanks / gratitude : __ morning __lunch/afternoon __evening
Today I'm grateful for / I give thanks for
1

2

3

Dear God, thank you…

Is there anything you want to show me?

I pray for…

ASK GOD TO BRING TO MIND A MEMORY

In my Tuesday night group we learned to ask God to show us things to appreciate. Each of us would be reminded of things long-forgotten. These include a garden swing and my basketball coach.

Try this exercise

Pray. Ask God to bring to mind a memory of something good.
See what comes to mind. If your mind goes blank, actively choose a positive memory and continue.
Bring the memory alive in your mind. In your mind's eye,
- What do you see? Look around and notice.
- What do you hear? What were you feeling?
- Who was with you at the time? What are they doing?
- Can you recall any sensations in your body?

Thank God for anything good.
- Ask him where he was and what he would like to show you.
- Ask God for insight into the memory.

Thank God for any insight. Would you like to say anything to him?

At some point consider,
- What are you sensing in your body now?
- What are you feeling now?
- Looking back, what are you grateful for?

Be sure to pray for those in the memory.

Finish by thanking God.

M T W T F S S   **DATE:** _____

Today I'm grateful for / I give thanks for

1

2

3

Dear God, thank you…

I pray for…

He is not here; he has risen! Remember how he told you, while he was still with you in Galilee. Luke 24:6 (NIV).

M T W T F S S   **DATE:** _____

Today I'm grateful for / I give thanks for

1

2

3

Dear God, thank you…

I pray for…

STEP 4 ENGAGE WITH YOUR GOD-MEMORIES

When we engage our God-memories we find it easier to re-engage with God in the present. Bring to mind a time when you experienced God, felt connected to Him, or felt joy, love etc.

Look at the boxes below if you believe that you have never experienced God. Many of us have experienced God more often than we realize.

Ask God to remind you of one of them, and then think about what you remember. Think about these experiences, thank God for them and spend some time journaling.

NOTICING AND NAMING OUR EXPERIENCES OF GOD

Most of us have had a sense of God or his leading in coming to faith or in reading the Bible.

For example, we have experienced him through

Salvation: in coming to faith.

Scripture: Has God ever spoken to you through the Bible?

Preachers/Speakers: Have you ever said, "I felt like they were speaking just to me"?

Time of worship / church service.

Silence.

Conviction of right and wrong.

Prompting for action.

Dreams / pictures.

Prayer times with God.

Spontaneous thoughts.

JOURNALING SPACE

I lie awake thinking of you, meditating on you through the night. Psalm 63:6 (NLT)

ENGAGING WITH A GOD MEMORY

A. Think of a time when you experienced God's presence, or felt connected to Him, or felt loved, protected, joy, etc. If you feel that you have not had an experience of God, then the box on the previous pages might help you recognize examples of when you hadn't realized it was God.

B. Think back to a time when you experienced God or when you were filled with feelings of love, joy, or peace.
Imagine who was there and what happened.

What was it like to be in God's presence or be led by him?
What do you see? Look around and notice…
What do you hear? What were you feeling?
Who was with you? Where are they?
What was happening in your body? Do you recall any sensations?
What did God show to you?

C. Savor the aspects of the experience that you appreciate the most. Go over it in your mind. There is a tiny step from being inside the memory of a previous experience of God to being inside a new one in the present. Often, this happens spontaneously. Ask yourself, "Does this feeling feel like it's in the past, or does it feel like he is here with me in the present?" As you ask this, often you will sense God with you. If not, ask him to help you perceive him with you.

God may bring to your mind thoughts, images and other content which are very subtle, but pay attention to your heart; sit with God and ask him what he wants to show you. Wait for Him.

D. Thank God for the memory, then ask him if there is anything he wants to show you. If he shows you something, then ask him a question and see what comes to mind or notice any changes in your body. We include this question in the Daily 1-2-3 pages from now on.
Keep doing steps B, C and D for as long as you like.

Make some notes and give the memory a two to five word title.

Pray for God to bless anyone else who was with you in the memory.

JOURNALING SPACE

For by grace you have been saved through faith. And this is not your own doing; it is the gift of God. Ephesians 2:8 (ESV)

REMEMBER THE DIFFERENCE YOUR CHRISTIAN FAITH MAKES

Without recollection, we forget. Faith needs occasional reminders, as 2 Peter says. If we don't, we will forget what God has already done. This affects our everyday lives. However, when we recall what God has done for us in the past, it changes the way we live in the present. By remembering the hope our faith gives, the love we feel, the chance to be part of a community, and the ecstasy / calming of worship, we can live with these perspectives in mind.

Writing things down in a journal or speaking them out loud in worship strengthens our faith more than thinking about them in our heads. Our brains work that way. Think about how your faith has changed your life. It makes a difference. Make a list. Say thank you to God. Other days, complete the Daily 1-2-3 page.

So I will always remind you of these things, even though you know them and are firmly established in the truth you now have. I think it is right to refresh your memory as long as I live in the tent of this body...Dear friends, this is now my second letter to you. I have written both of them as reminders to stimulate you to wholesome thinking. I want you to recall the words spoken in the past by the holy prophets and the command given by our Lord and Savior through your apostles. 2 Peter 1:12-13; 3:1-2 (NIV)

M T W T F S S   DATE: _____

Today I'm grateful for / I give thanks for

1

2

3

Dear God, thank you…

I pray for…

I thank my God every time I remember you. Philippians 1:3 (NIV).

M T W T F S S   DATE: _____

Today I'm grateful for / I give thanks for

1

2

3

Dear God, thank you…

I pray for…

WHAT IS SPECIAL ABOUT THE PEOPLE YOU APPRECIATE?

Earlier, you thought about the people around you and what you value about them. Now we take this a little further to consider what is *special* to you about them.

Consider the people around you and what you value about them. Begin with thinking what is good and distinctive about them?

Now build on that by thinking, What is there about them that makes them special to you?
- Is there a memory of them that reminds you of how special they are?
- Focus in on what makes them special to you.
- Do they know?
  Maybe ,
  - pray a prayer of thanksgiving for them or
  - send them a message to tell them what is special about them.

For example,
- you could be grateful for the kindness shown by a carer towards your elderly parents with Alzheimer's;
- you could be grateful that a mentor has opened a door for you;

- If you have close loving relationships, think what makes them special to you; if you do not feel close to them, look back and think of some special times.
  - Focus in on those times. This can lead you to feeling grateful and to prayer.

Today, think of some people you appreciate and you are grateful for. Write their names and describe what you appreciate / you are grateful for on the next page.

Now Jesus loved Martha and her sister and Lazarus. John 11:5 (NIV).

M T W T F S S   **DATE:** _____

Today I'm grateful for…

What makes them distinctive in a positive way is…

What makes them special to me is…

Do they know?
One thing I will do is…
- *You could write a note to tell them….*

Rejoice always, pray continually, give thanks in all circumstances; for this is God's will for you in Christ Jesus. 1 Thessalonians 5:16-18 (NIV).

M T W T F S S   **DATE:** _____

Today I'm grateful for…

What makes them distinctive in a positive way is…

What makes them special to me is…

Do they know?
One thing I will do is…
- *You could write a note to tell them….*

A CALM OR HAPPY MEMORY

1. Think of a time where you felt calm, happy, or peaceful.
- This can be a God memory if you like
- You can ask God to bring one to mind if you like

2. Imagine you are in that peaceful memory. Bring it alive by remembering how it felt, noticing your senses.
- What do you see? Look around and notice.
- What do you hear? What were you feeling?
- Who was with you? Where are they?
- What was happening in your body? Do you recall any sensations? *E.g. I feel the warmth of the sun on my face and arms.*

3. Notice what you are sensing in your body and what are you appreciating now as you recall the memory. *E.g. I sense the warm beams of sun on my arms and face. I remember feeling relaxed and thankful just to be with my family. I can feel this same relaxation and contentment in my body now.*

4. Thank God for the good things in that memory. Specifically, thank him for the good things you see, hear, and feel, etc.

5. Now ask God to show you where he is in the memory. If God is present everywhere, all-knowing and all-loving, then he was there in what you are remembering. So, ask him where he was and what he would like to show you.

What would you like to say to him?

M T W T F S S   **DATE:** _____

Today I'm grateful for / I give thanks for

1

2

3

Dear God, thank you...

I pray for...

The Lord your God is with you, the Mighty Warrior who saves. He will take great delight in you; in his love he will no longer rebuke you, but will rejoice over you with singing. Zephaniah 3:17 (NIV).

M T W T F S S   **DATE:** _____

Today I'm grateful for / I give thanks for

1

2

3

Dear God, thank you...

I pray for...

STEP 5 DO IT THROUGH THE DAY

It is fun to dive into a pool, glide elegantly, jump out, and repeat. Even so, spending a summer gliding is not the same as swimming. An open-water swimmer needs to learn the breaststroke or front crawl to live.

In the same way, occasionally giving thanks or being grateful is like diving, gliding, and leaping. By changing from being grateful and appreciative periodically to doing it regularly, you will maximize the benefits of this journal. You are at Step Six now. Doing it through the day.

This can help us

- Improve our mood;
- Become more relational;
- Connect with God;
- Improve our decisions;
- Thrive rather than survive;

The next step is to commit to three-times-a-day appreciation. This requires planning, but it is worth it! Try,

- Once in the morning
- Once at lunch / in the afternoon
- Once at night.

What is an easy way to start?

- Once, do this journal.
- Twice, pause for 30 seconds of giving thanks / gratitude without journaling..
- Use the Daily 1-2-3 pages to keep track. From now on, tick the new line:
  I spent time in giving thanks / gratitude:
  __ morning __lunch/afternoon __evening
- You can photocopy the double-spread on the next pages

PLANNING TO BE APPRECIATIVE

Spend a moment to think. When will you spend 30 seconds in appreciation?

- What will remind you?
- What will help you?
- What will stop you?
- What can you do about it?

I came to give life—life in all its fullness. John 10:10 (NCV).

EVERYDAY THINGS   DATE: _____

We can be thankful for everyday things. In your life today, name three you are thankful for.

1

2

3

Spend some time giving thanks to God for these things.

And he took bread, gave thanks and broke it, and gave it to them, saying, "This is my body given for you; do this in remembrance of me." Luke 22:19 (NIV).

EVERYDAY THINGS   DATE: _____

What everyday things would you miss if they were taken away? Write three things you take for granted.

1

2

3

Spend some time giving thanks to God for what you have.

You can photocopy the double-spread on the next pages.

M T W T F S S**DATE:** _____

I spent time giving thanks / gratitude : __ morning __lunch/afternoon __evening

Today I'm grateful for / I give thanks for

1

2

3

Dear God, thank you…

Is there anything you want to show me?

I pray for…

I have told you these things so that you will be filled with my joy. Yes, your joy will overflow! John 15:11 (NLT)

M T W T F S S**DATE:** _____

I spent time giving thanks / gratitude : __ morning __lunch/afternoon __evening

Today I'm grateful for / I give thanks for

1

2

3

Dear God, thank you…

Is there anything you want to show me?

I pray for…

M T W T F S S   **DATE:** _____

I spent time giving thanks / gratitude : __ morning __ lunch/afternoon __ evening
Today I'm grateful for / I give thanks for
1

2

3

Dear God, thank you…

Is there anything you want to show me?

I pray for…

And the peace of God, which transcends all understanding, will guard your hearts and your minds in Christ Jesus. Philippians 4:7 (NIV).

M T W T F S S   **DATE:** _____

I spent time giving thanks / gratitude : __ morning __ lunch/afternoon __ evening
Today I'm grateful for / I give thanks for
1

2

3

Dear God, thank you…

Is there anything you want to show me?

I pray for…

THROUGH THE DAY REVIEW

**Did you practice appreciation for 30 seconds three times yesterday (once with the journal and then two other times)?
If so, well done! If not, don't worry about it. What can you do differently today? Try prompts such as,**

- Set an alarm.
- Link giving thanks / gratitude to a regular activity.
- If you get road rage, then as you enter your vehicle, choose to think of things to appreciate;
- If work stress is a problem, spend 30 seconds in appreciation as you enter the vicinity of your office.
- You can link boiling the kettle, walking the dog, taking a shower, eating lunch
- When saying grace with a meal, you could ask your friends or family what they appreciate from the day.

AN APPRECIATION MEMORY

Ask God to bring to mind a good memory. You could ask him to remind you of may be a peaceful, a happy or an empowering memory. Bring it alive. Remember how it felt.

- What do you see? Look around and notice.
- What do you hear? What were you feeling?
- Who was with you? Where are they?
- What was happening in your body? Do you recall any sensations?

Thank God for these good things.

- Ask him where he was and what he would like to show you.
- Ask God for his insight into the memory.

Thank God for any insight. What would you like to say to him?

At some point consider,

- What are you sensing in your body?
- What are you feeling now?
- What are you grateful for as you look back?

Pray for anyone in the memory.
Finish by thanking God.

MORE STEPS TO FEELING GREAT

STEP 6 INTENTIONAL GRATITUDE

Getting intentional about gratitude can change your life. As you intentionally spend time in thanksgiving until you feel it and your mood changes. It also helps you to connect with God at the same time.

The Appreciation Cycle on the next page summarizes what we have done in the journal.

- Use it daily to build new brain pathways and change how you feel.
- Take a breather somewhere and go through the cycle.
- Make some notes below on how it goes.
- Use it alongside the other exercises in this journal.

APPRECIATION CYCLE

This summarizes what we have done in this journal.

1. **Bring to mind something that is good or ask God to show you one.** This may be an experience of God, something special, or something very normal. **Don't go with a memory that has associations with something negative. If it is negative, choose a different memory.**
2. **Notice** (and write down if you can) **what you are sensing in your body and what are you feeling now.**
3. **Bring to mind a specific memory that connects to what you are thankful for.** Dwell on the memory. Bring it to life.
   - What do you see? Look around and notice.
   - What do you hear? What were you feeling?
   - Who was with you? Where are they?
   - What happened?
   - What was happening in your body? Do you recall any sensations?
   - What did God show to you?
4. **Thank God.**
5. **Savor the highlights.** Chew them over. Zoom in on them and see them in bright colors. Thank God for them.
6. **Ask God if he wants to show you anything about the good thing.**
   Give God some time to reveal himself to you. God may bring to your mind thoughts, images and other content which are very subtle, but pay attention to your heart; sit with God and ask him what he wants to show you. Wait for Him.
   Experiencing God in the present is a tiny step from envisioning a previous divine encounter. This can happen when you ask yourself, "Does this feeling feel like it's in the past, or does it feel like he is here with me in the present?" Often you will then sense God with you now. If you don't then ask him to help you perceive him with you. Ask him if there is anything he wants to show you in the present.
7. **Repeat steps 2-6 until you feel a difference in your body and you feel / are in a state of gratitude**.
8. **Write**
   - A short title;
   - Some details to stimulate your memory in the future;
   - What you sense in your body now;
   - What the Lord showed you;
   - The title in the Appreciation Memories List at the back of the journal.
9. **Pray for anyone who has come to mind.**
10. **Optional: Find a relevant photo and stick it in this journal to remind you.**

"DO YOU REMEMBER WHEN?" SHARING STORIES WITH THOSE WHO MEAN THE MOST TO YOU

Stories brighten conversations and build relationships. Combined with appreciation, they can enrich any relationship. When families share positive stories about each other, their relationships become stronger. I was thinking about this earlier today.

I asked Ruth, "Do you remember when you, Alex, and Chris cheered me on during the steepest part of the Lilleshall 10K? It was great to see you. That gave me a boost." Her response was "oh, that's nice." Life continued, but our connection was strengthened by the story.

EXERCISE: "DO YOU REMEMBER WHEN?..."

Use my simple story as a model.
- Think about someone you care about
- Recall a positive experience you had with them
- Turn it into a "do you remember when," or "I was thinking about " story.
- Keep it short: 2 to 3 minutes. When sharing about our lives, short stories work well. This lets the other person in on the conversation faster.
- Intentionally share this story to build your connection with the person you love.

A glad heart makes a cheerful face. Proverbs 15:13 (ESV).

M T W T F S S   DATE: _____

I spent time giving thanks / gratitude : __ morning __lunch/afternoon __evening
Today I'm grateful for / I give thanks for
1

2

3

Dear God, thank you…

Is there anything you want to show me?

I pray for…

For I know the plans I have for you, declares the Lord, plans for welfare and not for evil, to give you a future and a hope. Jeremiah 29:11 (ESV).

M T W T F S S   DATE: _____

I spent time giving thanks / gratitude : __ morning __lunch/afternoon __evening
Today I'm grateful for / I give thanks for
1

2

3

Dear God, thank you…

Is there anything you want to show me?

I pray for…

CHANGING RELATIONSHIPS BY APPRECIATING OTHERS

Think & write down
- Who is most special to you?
- What do you appreciate about them?
- What are you grateful for?
- What would life be like without them?
- Are you developing too intimate a relationship with someone who is not yours? Get off the escalator! Think about someone else.

Thank
- Thank God for them. If there are positive memories with them, bring them to mind.

Pray
- Pray for them
- Ask God where he is in the relationship and ask him if there is anything he wants to show you.

Act:
- Appreciate these special people practically rather than take them for granted.
- Can you tell them how special they are to you?

Notice
- If your spouse or partner is not listed.
  - Name three things you appreciate about them. When a friend did this with a couple it took an hour for them to find three things but that was a breakthrough.
  - Go out of your way over the next month to tell them what you appreciate about them. Go the extra mile even if part of you does not want to do it. Research shows that this makes a massive difference.
  - Pray that God blesses them.
  - Do something positive for them.

Jesus looked at him and loved him. "One thing you lack," he said. "Go, sell everything you have and give to the poor, and you will have treasure in heaven. Then come, follow me." Mark 10:21 (NIV).

M T W T F S S   **DATE:** _____

I spent time giving thanks / gratitude : __ morning __lunch/afternoon __evening
Today I'm grateful for / I give thanks for
1

2

3

Dear God, thank you…

Is there anything you want to show me?

I pray for…

I thought about the former days, the years of long ago; I remembered my songs in the night. My heart meditated and my spirit asked. Psalm 77:5-6 (NIV).

M T W T F S S   **DATE:** _____

I spent time giving thanks / gratitude : __ morning __lunch/afternoon __evening
Today I'm grateful for / I give thanks for
1

2

3

Dear God, thank you…

Is there anything you want to show me?

I pray for…

ENRICHING YOUR FAMILY RELATIONSHIPS

Think:
- Write the names of your family members.
- Rate the warmth of your relationship with them from 0 (low) to 10 (high). There is no shame here. This is for your eyes only.
- Write what is distinctive and positive about them.
- Write what is special to you about them (if anything).
- What would life be like without them?

Thank
- Thank God for them. Recall specific memories and use the Appreciation Cycle.

Pray:
- Pray for them
- Ask God where he is in the relationship and ask him if there is anything he wants to show you.

Act:
- Appreciate these special people practically rather than take them for granted.
- Can you share with any of them how special they are to you?

And so we know and rely on the love God has for us. God is love. Whoever lives in love lives in God, and God in them. This is how love is made complete among us so that we will have confidence on the day of judgment: In this world we are like Jesus. There is no fear in love. But perfect love drives out fear, because fear has to do with punishment. The one who fears is not made perfect in love. 1 John 4:16-18 (NIV).

M T W T F S S   **DATE:** _____

I spent time giving thanks / gratitude : __ morning __lunch/afternoon __evening
Today I'm grateful for / I give thanks for
1

2

3

Dear God, thank you…

Is there anything you want to show me?

I pray for…

is right, whatever is pure, whatever is lovely, whatever is admirable – if anything is excellent or praiseworthy – think about such things. Philippians 4:8 (NIV).

M T W T F S S   **DATE:** _____

I spent time giving thanks / gratitude : __ morning __lunch/afternoon __evening
Today I'm grateful for / I give thanks for
1

2

3

Dear God, thank you…

Is there anything you want to show me?

I pray for…

BRINGING APPRECIATION INTO MARRIAGE OR PARTNERSHIP

THREE EASY WINS

- First, ask your partner what they appreciated from their day. This is preferable to, "What are you grateful for?" or the dreaded, "How was work?" If your partner is in overwhelm, this can be tricky. Don't push the point. Many couples find this helpful.
- Second, one of the first people I taught appreciation to finishes every day with his wife. They describe three things they appreciate every night. This helps their relationship and improves their sleep. Chris Coursey developed this into the 3x3x3 exercise you can read below.
- Third, tell a life-sharing story. If you have done an appreciation exercise, tell a two minutes story about it.

ESTABLISH A ROUTINE

Coursey and Wilder have thought about applying appreciation to marriage. They find that appreciation is often the hidden ingredient that determines if a marriage is strong or weak. The brain that is trained on appreciation will scan the environment for good things, but if you don;t do that its easy to be critical and find fault in other people.

To train your brain in marriage they suggest you.

Maintain a steady diet of the following activities:

• Verbalize the qualities you enjoy about your spouse.

• Continue to hug, cuddle, and kiss like you mean it.

• Let your face light up when you see your spouse. Use your voice to convey the love you feel for your beloved.

• Take a hot bath or a shower together. Use your words and touch to express how much you enjoy the one you love.

M T W T F S S   **DATE:** _____

I spent time giving thanks / gratitude : __ morning __lunch/afternoon __evening
Today I'm grateful for / I give thanks for
1

2

3

Dear God, thank you…

Is there anything you want to show me?

I pray for…

Peace I leave with you; my peace I give to you. Not as the world gives do I give to you. Let not your hearts be troubled, neither let them be afraid. John 14:27 (ESV)

M T W T F S S   **DATE:** _____

I spent time giving thanks / gratitude : __ morning __lunch/afternoon __evening
Today I'm grateful for / I give thanks for
1

2

3

Dear God, thank you…

Is there anything you want to show me?

I pray for…

BRINGING APPRECIATION INTO MARRIAGE OR PARTNERSHIP

WRITE A LETTER.

Marcus Warner (page 93) says,

One week when Brenda was out of town for several days, I found it hard to fall asleep. I decided to write her a letter. In the letter, I wrote out some of the things I appreciated about her. The letter went something like this. I know I can be distant and make you feel unappreciated, but really, nearly every good thing in my life today has its roots in you. You are the adventurous one. You planned surprise birthday vacations for me, you made sure we had extended family trips in the mountains, you always find ways to make the home more beautiful. I tend to complain about the money and rob some of the joy by focusing on the cost. But as I sit here alone, missing you, I realize how much richness you add to my life. My best memories all involve you. Your passion for life and willingness to spend something to make those memories has made our lives better.

Writing a letter like this now and then can help you remember what there is to appreciate about the person you married. Just remembering that you appreciate someone and dwelling on that appreciation strengthens the bond between you.

(c) Lists. Take the list-making approach we have used in this journal and write about memories with your partner. For example,

- Make a top five list of character qualities you appreciate, then find a story that embodies each quality and write about it.

Do the same with

- Vacation memories
- Holiday memories
- Memories of realizing you were falling in love
- Romantic memories after the honeymoon
- Joyful parenting memories

Six sets of memories with five stories in each gives you 30 joyful memories to fuel your appreciation of the other person. Write these out, give them titles, and keep them handy so that when you are struggling to remember what you appreciate about your spouse, you can pull out the lists and spend some time remembering what you appreciate.

It is a good idea to make lists when you feel connected and relational. These lists then become tools you can refer to in order to help regain perspective when you do get upset.

3X3X3. BY CHRIS COURSEY (PAGE 96-98)

- *Here is what Jen and I practice. First, Jen my wife and I take turns sharing three things from our day that we appreciate.*

- *Second, we express three qualities we appreciate about each other, including examples of these qualities "in action."*

- *Finally, we highlight three qualities we appreciate about God, again using examples. (You could also insert another topic of your choosing here.)*

Each step looks like this:

- *Appreciation about my day: "I enjoyed my walk this afternoon. It felt so good to get outside and move around. The birds were singing, and the breeze was refreshing ..."*

- *Appreciation about my spouse: "I really appreciate your heart for hospitality. When our friend Helen came over this evening, you worked hard to prepare a meal that she would enjoy. I like how you care about the people in our life!"*

- *Appreciation about God: "I am thankful for God's patience with me. I feel like God continues to give me opportunities to grow which makes me feel loved."*

The first night we tried this exercise while snuggling in bed. The effects of the interaction were immediate and profound, which surprised both of us.

During the exercise, I could feel Jen's body begin to relax and her breathing slow down. By the end, both of us were smiling and feeling peaceful. The exercise took about ten minutes to complete. Within another ten minutes, Jen was fast asleep for the night.

This ended up being one of the best nights of sleep she had in a long time. For years, we have used this exercise to close our day. Every time, Jen falls asleep within minutes instead of hours. Don't simply take my word for the value of this exercise; try it yourself, and watch what happens!

Gracious words are like a honeycomb, sweetness to the soul and health to the body. Proverbs 16:24 (ESV)

STEP 7 CHANGING YOUR WORLD

The last step is to keep growing in appreciation and change the world round you.

- My workplace and church are happier as I have brought appreciation intentionally into meetings that I chair and 360 degrees of my interactions.
- As an imperfect leader, the people who feel appreciated by me are likely to forgive my flaws, while those who feel unappreciated are likely to pull back from me.
- As I go through my day, part of living as a Christian is to be a person of peace and appreciation. It costs nothing and opens doors all over the place.
- It also increases my happiness and contentment. As Philippians 4:11-13 puts it, "I have learned to be content whatever the circumstances. I know what it is to be in need, and I know what it is to have plenty. I have learned the secret of being content in any and every situation, whether well fed or hungry, whether living in plenty or in want. I can do all this through him who gives me strength." Being thankful and gratitude open the door to being with God in our difficult circumstances. As we spend time with God and pass on the blessings from him, so the atmosphere around us changes.

Give it a go! There are lots of other ways to pass on the benefits of what we are doing. I suggest you pick out the most interesting parts of this section. Do not do them in order.

Many people find the Three Times-A-Day for 30 Days Challenge, on the next few pages, transformational.

THREE TIMES-A-DAY FOR 30 DAYS CHALLENGE

We emphasized spending time in giving thanks and gratitude throughout the day. It took me months to turn thankfulness into a habit. Gradually, I moved from doing individual exercises, to doing something daily, to being more regular, to doing it three-times-a-day to it being a natural regular part of my life.

By now, if you have done the exercises in this book, you will have built up your experience of appreciation and you are ready to try the 30 Day Challenge:

- For 30 days, try having three times of giving thanks / gratitude each day.
    - Once in the morning,
    - once at lunch / in the afternoon
    - once at night
- In at least one of these use the Appreciation Cycle

With a little thought and planning, this can work. It will take time to build the habit, but it is worth it. It can rewire your brain. As Dr Jim Wilder says, "our brains have a default emotional state—the state it sits in when other emotions are not temporarily overwhelming it. In the first eighteen months of life, the default emotional state in our brains, which should be joy, is set to one of the six unpleasant emotions that the brain recognizes—sadness, fear, anger, shame, disgust, and hopeless despair. This was not a choice you made. It was set according to what was happening in your life during your infancy. **Here is the good news: we can reset our default emotional state to joy. This happens in our brains as a response to repeated exposure to a state of gratitude**" (p217). Dr Wilder recommends the Three Times a Day for Thirty Days Challenge because it works!

PREPARATION

- Create a list of 5-10 appreciation memories that you have found as you have worked through this journal. Put the list in the *Appreciation Memories List* at the back of the book. Give each memory a short title, e.g. 'Bluebell Woods'.
- Decide what time of day you will spend a longer period doing some appreciation and when you will do the shorter times.
- Consider an alarm or another prompt, such as linking appreciation / gratitude to a regular activity.
    - If you get road rage, then as you enter your vehicle, choose to think of things to appreciate;
    - If work stress is a problem, spend 30 seconds in appreciation as you enter the vicinity of your office.

A glad heart makes a cheerful face. Proverbs 15:13 (ESV)

- You can link boiling the kettle, walking the dog, taking a shower, eating lunch
  - When saying grace with a meal, you could ask your friends or family what they appreciate from the day.
- Many people find it easiest to do this with a friend. Why not do it in a small group or with a friend?
- Some couples share things to appreciate from their day to anchor thankfulness in their routine and as part of the 30 Day challenge.

HOW TO DO THE CHALLENGE
For the longer period
1. Spend a couple of minutes calming down in your usual way, or if you find that difficult, slow your breathing down and exhale for longer than your inhale. If you would like to learn more about calming and finding peace, see our course at www.joyskills.online
2. Spend 3-5 minutes in giving thanks / gratitude. Use the Appreciation Cycle.
   Begin by focusing on your first appreciation memory. Fully enter that memory, remembering how you felt in your body and emotions, and what you saw, heard, smelled, tasted, and touched . You may like to use a photo or an object as a prompt. Continue using the cycle for this memory until your time runs out or your sense of "being there" fades.
   Then, go to another memory on your list. Again, fully enter. Keep going until you have spent five minutes. Every time the sense of "being there" fades, move to the next memory.
3. Make notes.
4. When you have finished, it's helpful to share one of these memories with someone who is glad to be with you. This helps grow your joy levels.

For the other two times
Use any of the exercises in the book. If you use the Daily 1-2-3 pages, they will help you keep track.

NOTES
- Make any notes that help you do this exercise.
- Use the 30 Day Tracker on the next page to help develop this habit.
- You can photocopy the double spread of Daily 1-2-3 pages on the next pages if that would be useful.

For from him and through him and for him are all things. To him be the glory forever! Amen. Rom 11:36. (NIV).

30 DAY TRACKER

Day	Tick Sessions			Notes
	1	2	3	
1				
2				
3				
4				
5				
6				
7				
8				
9				
10				
11				
12				
13				
14				
15				
16				
17				
18				
19				
20				
21				
22				
23				
24				
25				
26				
27				
28				
29				
30				

M T W T F S S   **DATE:** _____

I spent time giving thanks / gratitude : __ morning __lunch/afternoon __evening
Today I'm grateful for / I give thanks for
1

2

3

Dear God, thank you…

Is there anything you want to show me?

I pray for…

I have told you these things so that you will be filled with my joy. Yes, your joy will overflow! John 15:11 (NLT)

M T W T F S S   **DATE:** _____

I spent time giving thanks / gratitude : __ morning __lunch/afternoon __evening
Today I'm grateful for / I give thanks for
1

2

3

Dear God, thank you…

Is there anything you want to show me?

I pray for…

M T W T F S S   **DATE:** _____

I spent time giving thanks / gratitude : __ morning __ lunch/afternoon __ evening
Today I'm grateful for / I give thanks for
1

2

3

Dear God, thank you…

Is there anything you want to show me?

I pray for…

And the peace of God, which transcends all understanding, will guard your hearts and your minds in Christ Jesus. Philippians 4:7 (NIV).

M T W T F S S   **DATE:** _____

I spent time giving thanks / gratitude : __ morning __ lunch/afternoon __ evening
Today I'm grateful for / I give thanks for
1

2

3

Dear God, thank you…

Is there anything you want to show me?

I pray for…

IDEAS FOR GROWTH

Over the next pages, I give you some ideas to focus on. Choose the ones which will help you. Don't go through this part in order.

ENGAGING WITH A GOD MEMORY

A. As you grow in appreciation, Keep engaging with your God memories.

B. Ask God to remind you of them or think
back to a time when you experienced God or when you were filled with feelings of love, joy, or peace.
Imagine who was there and what happened.

- What was it like to be in God's presence or be led by him?
- What do you see? Look around and notice…
- What do you hear? What were you feeling?
- Who was with you? Where are they?
- What was happening in your body? Do you recall any sensations?
- What did God show to you?

C. Savor the aspects of the experience that you appreciate the most. Go over it in your mind. There is a tiny step from being inside the memory of a previous experience of God to being inside a new one in the present. Often, this happens spontaneously. Ask yourself, "Does this feeling feel like it's in the past, or does it feel like he is here with me in the present?" As you ask this, often you will sense God with you. If not, ask him to help you perceive him with you.

God may bring to your mind thoughts, images and other content which are very subtle, but pay attention to your heart; sit with God and ask him what he wants to show you. Wait for Him.

D. Thank God for the memory, then ask him if there is anything he wants to show you. If he shows you something, then ask him a question and see what comes to mind or notice any changes in your body.

- Keep doing steps B, C and D for as long as you like.
- Make some notes and give the memory a two to five word title.
- Pray for God to bless anyone with you in the memory.

CHANGING RELATIONSHIPS BY REMINDING YOURSELF WHO CARES FOR YOU

We begin by looking backwards. Think,

- Who is always there for you?
- Who listens to you?
- Who has helped you become the person you are today?
- Who loves you?

Appreciate these special people rather than take them for granted.

You can tell them you appreciate them.

Remember, this all has to be genuine. Don't be phony.

Notice people's positive qualities (what is distinctive and good) and think about what makes them special to you.

Enjoy them!

REMINISCING

Think of a positive story about someone.

Write <u>one sentence</u> about what was happening.
For example, "Do you remember when …"

Write in some detail what happened when the person did something positive

Write the difference it made.

Share this with them. Maybe verbally or in a message.
"I was so grateful / thankful that you…."

Pray for the Lord to bless them.

> *Know therefore that the Lord your God is God; he is the faithful God, keeping his covenant of love to a thousand generations of those who love him and keep his commandments. Deuteronomy 7:9 (NIV).*

MULTIPLYING YOUR IMPACT THROUGH STORIES

Crafting stories from our lives

- help us notice more about our experience and clarify the essential parts.
- help us understand our history and put together the pieces of our lives.
- improve our relationships as we learn to tell stories long enough to be interesting, but not so long that people want to escape our company.
- help integrate, captivate, influence, and transform and help us get our point across in any situation. People in all walks of life will listen to a story–and will love it–if they feel it applies to what we have talked about.
- help leaders bring culture change. If you want to grow appreciation in your organization or church then do the exercises and tell stories.
- **help everyone can have a good time. What's not to like! As we have said before, if you have gained anything from this journal and want to share it with others, an effective way of doing so is through storytelling.**

HOW LIFE SHARING WORKS

You can share stories about your life in different ways to grow happiness around you and make people feel glad to be together with you. You can,

- Tell a positive story about someone to thank them… this can begin with, "Do you remember when…", and include a "I was so grateful / thankful that you…."
- Tell a story about how spending time in appreciation helped you. This could be something like, "I was feeling bad about going into a meeting and I knew it would affect the atmosphere. So I spent five minutes thinking about what I appreciate about the people in the meeting. This changed my interaction with folks and I realized my eye contact was better with people I dislike and we avoided the resistance that would have happened if I had been less positive towards people."
- Tell a story about using one of the exercises.
- Tell a God-story.

EXERCISE: SHARING FROM YOUR LIFE WITHOUT OVERWHELMING PEOPLE

Remember the goal. This exercise helps you pass on your learning so that others have a model of how to do it and what its benefits are.

1. **Choose one thing to share about**

   You can
   - Tell a positive story about someone to thank them… this can begin with, "Do you remember when …", and include a "I was so grateful / thankful that you…."
   - Tell a story about using one of the exercises.
   - Tell a story about an experience of God.
   - Speak about a time that spending time in appreciation helped you.
   - Talk about anything else that comes to mind now that you would like to share.

2. **Describe in one sentence what was happening. This should be <u>one sentence without pain</u>.** Do not go into detail.
   Write your sentence here…

3. **Describe in as much detail as possible what happened as you spent time in thankfulness or gratitude / met with God / did the exercise, etc.**
   Prompts for your thinking are:
   - How did you do it?
   - What exactly did you do? Did you journal? Do an exercise? Pray? Do it with someone else etc.?
   - Was it is a person, place, pet you were grateful for?
   - Did you feel anything in your body?
   - What emotions did you feel?
   - Did the Lord say anything?

   Write your description here…

Grace to you and peace from God the Father and the Lord Jesus Christ. 2 Thessalonians 1:2 (NIV).

Describe the difference it made. This is key in helping people understand the impact on you of what happened

4. **Edit your writing.**
   - Here you cut down your notes and write what happened in a paragraph or two to last 2-3 minutes. Bear in mind
     - Keep it short.
     - No pain.
     - No humor.
     - What happened?
     - What difference did it make?
   - Read it out and time yourself. Is it less than a minute? You need more detail. Is it over 3 minutes? If so, cut it down because people are likely to stop listening before you finish.

Write your paragraphs here

5. **Sharing.**
   - Practice sharing for **two to three minutes** with someone who you know well. For some people this will feel too short and for others it will feel like an eternity.
   - Keep practicing.

BRINGING APPRECIATION OF OTHERS INTO YOUR PRAYER LIFE

- Ask God to bring to mind positive things about people as you pray.
- Ask God, What is there to appreciate about them?
- Do this as you obey Christ's command to pray for your enemies. (I am not suggesting that you get close to people who damage you).
- Extend this time if you desire to improve a relationship.

As the Father has loved me, so have I loved you. Now remain in my love. If you keep my commands, you will remain in my love, just as I have kept my Father's commands and remain in his love. John 15:9-10 (NIV).

BRINGING CELEBRATION AND THANKFULNESS INTO MEETINGS, EVENTS AND YOUR ORGANIZATION'S CULTURE

My sister told me a true story of a volunteer who, when given a bunch of flowers, said "that will keep me going for another year." A simple act of appreciation was fuel for a year of service. Yesterday I was told of someone who was upset because though they had been thanked profusely for one thing, they had not been thanked for another. Their "appreciation tank" was empty, and I hadn't noticed.

I wonder how you can bring thankfulness into

- Some of your meetings
- Some of your events
- Some parts of your organization's culture

Spend some time in prayer and ask God about it.

This is the day that the Lord has made; let us rejoice and be glad in it.
Psalm 118:24 (ESV).

CREATING HIGHLIGHTS

"Please describe one of your happy memories" asked Meik Wiking (2019, p.10). People recalled experiences that were
- novel,
- meaningful,
- emotional, and
- engaged the senses.

Nearly two-thirds of memories involved several senses, and a third were meaningful experiences such as weddings and births. A quarter of them were unusual experiences, such as visiting a country for the first time.

Think about the next year.
What highlights could you create?
How can you add happiness to your memories?
- This week?
- On trips?
- At other times?

Wiking suggests you add a little more
- Attention to what is happening (100%* of the happy memories had this)
- Multi-sensory experience (over ½ of the happy memories had this);
- Emotion (50%*);
- Storytelling (1/3*);
- Meaning (1/3*);
- Novelty & extraordinary events (1/4*);
- Peaks & struggle (1/4*);
- Photo-taking and, diary-making and memento- shopping. (7%*).

Pray about this and ask God if there is anything he wants to show you.

*The % is the % of recalled memories that had this factor.

Six days later Jesus took Peter and the two brothers, James and John, and led them up a high mountain to be alone. 2 As the men watched, Jesus' appearance was transformed so that his face shone like the sun, and his clothes became as white as light. Matthew 17:1-2 (NLT).

IMPROVING THE ATMOSPHERE OF DIFFICULT MEETINGS OR CONVERSATIONS

Do you have a meeting coming up which you feel negative about?*

Think about the meeting. If it is with someone that you have a negative attitude towards, but they are not emotionally or physically dangerous for you, then try this exercise.

Spend time in appreciation.

(1) Bring to mind positives about the person (if it's a one-on-one), or people who will be present.

(2) Spend time in thankfulness until you feel it in your body.

(3) Pray and ask God for wisdom and peace to calm your heart and emotions.

(4) Pray for participants and the outcomes of the meeting.

(5) Ask God if he wants to show you anything.

Prior to the meeting, slow your breathing and pause for a moment of appreciation.

In the meeting, try to get relational before doing your work. Use the simple process from Rare Leadership in the Workplace by Warner & Wilder,

- Look people in the eyes;
- Express curiosity;
- Go about your work;
- Smile!

*This is not advice for preparing for meetings with violent, abusive or narcissistic people.

"Above all, love each other deeply, because love covers over a multitude of sins." 1 Peter 4:8 (NIV).

CONGRATULATIONS
YOU MADE IT!

I appreciate your time and effort in getting to this page. Because of completing the 7 steps, you deserve a pat on the back or hug.

Take a moment to browse your journal. Give God thanks for what you have done and the journey you have taken. Ask yourself,

- What have I learned through this journal?
- What do I want to take away from my appreciation journey?
- Did I achieve my goals?
- Would I like to adopt any new habits?
- What lies at the heart of what I have written?
- What comes to mind regularly in the Daily 1-2-3 pages? Are they similar to the topical lists?
- Who comes to mind regularly? Do they know how special they are to you?

- Turn this reflection into prayer.

CONTINUING THE JOURNEY

THE GOOD IN MY LIFE RIGHT NOW

WHAT IS THE BEST THING ABOUT YOUR LIFE NOW?

1. **Bring to mind something that is good or ask God to show you one.** This may be to bring to mind something about your relationship with God, something special or something every day. *For example, I think of regularly playing sport with my friend Andy.*
2. **Thank God for them.** *I give thanks for Andy and the relaxation and companionship we have.*
3. **Bring to mind a specific memory that connects to what you are thankful for.** *I give thanks for the time Andy brought my son and me for my son's first half round of golf.*
4. **Ask God if he wants to show you anything about the good thing.** *The Lord shows me that this is the multi-generational community I have been trying to build; it is a pleasant memory and also a sign of things to come.*
5. **Ask God to help you perceive him right now.** *I feel a deep calm in my body and a sense of God's peace. I ask the Lord to be more aware of him and more aware of how I am functioning and relating with others.*
6. **Focus on the highlights / the best bits of what you are thankful for.** Savor them and turn them over in your mind. Bring them to life as much as you can. Thank God for them. *I turn over in my mind the memory of Chris hitting his first golf shot and then Andy helping him with his second shot. I give thanks for how special Chris, my son, and Alex, my daughter, are to me. I remember a scene on Warden Hill, overlooking Luton, and think of the time the three of us were walking together. I spend some time in thankfulness.*
7. **Repeat steps 4-6 until you feel a difference in your body and you feel / are in a state of gratitude**. . Keep going as long as you like then finish by praying about anything that emerges. *I feel the difference as a sense of peace, a lightness in my chest, a smile returning, becoming more relational or feeling happier and similar things. I pray for the Lord to bless Andy and Chris, who is sitting for an exam at the moment. The Lord then speaks to me about my own life.*
8. **Write:** A title for this reflection *[I called it Andy with Chris- first golf]*; Some details to help recall it in the future; What you sense in your body now; What the Lord showed you.
   Put the title in the Index of Appreciation Memories at the back of the journal.
9. **Pray for any people you have thought of.**
10. **Optional: If you have a photo, print it and stick it in this journal to remind you of this.**

LOOKING TO THE FUTURE

What happy memories will you create in the next six months?
What happy memories will you create in the next 48 hours?

Activity 1. The next 48 hours: Create happier memories in normal life by sharing joy in your day: creating a new habit:

Sharing joy: people feel joy when they connect with someone whose face and voice tell them they are happy to be with them. Smiling, a warm tone, eye contact and giving people surprises can pass joy on. To build happier memories into normal activities try,

- Smiling & letting your eyes light up when you greet those you love;
- Using a warm tone of voice & touching when appropriate;
- Giving surprises that make eyes light up;
- Telling and hearing stories about happy memories;
- Music;
- Appreciation;
- Doing what you can to end interactions positively;
- Synchronizing with others - being glad to be with people in their highs or lows, helping them feel validated and comforted;
- Interacting with food or drink.

GIVING ATTENTION TO YOUR DAY WITH GOD

What will be at the heart of your day?

Ask yourself,

- What will be at the heart of my day?
- What are my priorities this week?
- Do I like what I see?

- If your next 24 hours feel functional, ask yourself whether they reflect your values and what you want to do with your life?

- Spend some time in appreciation and reflection.

- Ask God how you can bring joy into your week. As you look back on your week, what will bring you joy and gratitude?

LOOKING BACK: PHOTO ACTIVITIES

Activity 1: For you - remembering your memories.

Fast: Search online for some of your favorite places. What feelings surface from the photos? What memories?

Takes longer: Go to your own photos, maybe on social media or on your computer. Look at them. What feelings surface from the photos? What memories? Consider putting them as your desktop or in other places where you might see them often, e.g. phone screen saver, or frame some and display them near your favorite spots at home or work.

Activity 2: Adding photos or memorabilia to the journal entries you have already done.
Review your journal entries and if there any particularly meaningful ones, print out a photo that relates to them and stick them in this journal. *For example, I had a photo of Chris with Andy (on the previous page) and I printed it and stuck it in the journal. Now when I use the journal that image propels me back to the memory.*

Activity 3: Reminiscing by telling funny stories that emerge from the photos.

Reminiscing with others who are interested is good for us and helps others grow their identity as we tell our stories. What funny stories emerge as you look at the photos. Rather than sharing 25 photos with little detail (which only engages people's left side of the brain); consider telling one story that emerges from a photo.

For example, I enjoy prompting my father to tell stories such as Victory in Europe Day (where as a 17-year-old he climbed up a lamppost in the middle up roaring crowds in Trafalgar Square) rather than looking at too many photos.

Activity 4: Reminiscing by asking people about the stories that emerge from photos.

If you are with a family member, consider asking them about a photo and see what you find out. You can ask about the funniest or most memorable time your family member had with the person in the photo (or what was eccentric about them).

The eccentricity question is a great open question. I've heard of grannies going round Europe with revolvers in their suitcase hunting Nazis, about Winston Churchill's secretaries, granddads who went to bed with chocolate under their pillows! It can bring laughter and a lightness of touch into everyday conversations.

YOUR FAVORITE MOVIES, TV SHOWS, AND COMEDY CLIPS

Do you have a favorite movie, TV show or comedy clip that makes you smile?
- Write some of them below. What do you appreciate about them?
- What is distinctive and good about them?
- Why not watch one of them and thank God for laughter?

One person I know was "prescribed comedy" for a month. She watched something she found funny every day and her mood improved.

PEOPLE WHO INVESTED IN YOU

Consider the people who invested in you.
- What was unique about them?
- What was special-to-you about them?
- Is there a memory about them you cherish?
- Are they aware? Maybe,
    - Say a prayer of thanksgiving for them
    - Let them know how much you appreciate them with a message.

YOUR FAVORITE FOOD AND DRINK

Remembering the routine things we enjoy is good. As you go about your day, give thanks for the little things.
- At mealtimes, many Christians pray a prayer of thanksgiving (or grace). Consider doing that.
- Is there anything you haven't eaten or drank in a while that you enjoy and wouldn't take you down a negative avenue?
- Bring to mind the happiest meals you have eaten.
    - What company did you have? Are there any memories you have of them?
    - Give thanks to God for them
    - What could you do to make future meals more joyful?

Relationship builder:
Discuss a meal you shared with your partner, your child, a parent, a friend, etc. Tell them about a meal you enjoyed together. Let them know what made it special. We build relationships over food and drink, so why not use the reminiscing time as an opportunity to do something together again?

REVIEWING WITH GOD

Sometimes I remember things from the previous week. Whenever I do, I ask God about the significance of the memory. Usually, he gives me insight into my past and re-frames it. I'll often feel gratitude, peace, and a sense of his presence.

After taking the cup, he gave thanks. Luke 22:17 (NIV).

REFERENCES

Warner, Marcus; Coursey, Chris M.. The 4 Habits of Joy-Filled Marriages (pp. 91-92). Moody Publishers. Kindle Edition.

Warner, M & Wilder J (2021) Rare Leadership in the Workplace. Northfield: Chicago.

Wiking, Meik (2019). The Art of Making Happy Memories. Penguin Life.

Wilder, J & Hendricks, M, The Other Half of Church, Moody Publishers. Kindle Edition.

NOTES & IDEAS

NOTES & IDEAS

APPRECIATION MEMORIES LIST

APPRECIATION MEMORIES LIST

Look back over the reviews that you have completed and write your favorite things that you appreciate and are grateful for on the next few pages.

Choose ones that evoke the most gratitude for you.

Summarize each entry with a title with 2-5 words in it.

APPRECIATION MEMORIES LIST CONTINUED

APPRECIATION CYCLE

This summarizes what we have done in this journal.

1. **Bring to mind something that is good or ask God to show you one.** This may be an experience of God, something special, or something very normal. **Don't go with a memory that has associations with something negative. If it is negative, choose a different memory.**
2. **Notice** (and write down if you can) **what you are sensing in your body and what are you feeling now.**
3. **Bring to mind a specific memory that connects to what you are thankful for.** Dwell on the memory. Bring it to life.
   - What do you see? Look around and notice.
   - What do you hear? What were you feeling?
   - Who was with you? Where are they?
   - What happened?
   - What was happening in your body? Do you recall any sensations?
   - What did God show to you?
4. **Thank God.**
5. **Savor the highlights.** Chew them over. Zoom in on them and see them in bright colors. Thank God for them.
6. **Ask God if he wants to show you anything about the good thing.**
   Give God some time to reveal himself to you. God may bring to your mind thoughts, images and other content which are very subtle, but pay attention to your heart; sit with God and ask him what he wants to show you. Wait for Him.
   Experiencing God in the present is a tiny step from envisioning a previous divine encounter. This can happen when you ask yourself, "Does this feeling feel like it's in the past, or does it feel like he is here with me in the present?" Often you will then sense God with you now. If you don't then ask him to help you perceive him with you. Ask him if there is anything he wants to show you in the present.
7. **Repeat steps 2-6 until you feel a difference in your body and you feel / are in a state of gratitude**.
8. **Write**
   - A short title;
   - Some details to stimulate your memory in the future;
   - What you sense in your body now;
   - What the Lord showed you;
   - The title in the Appreciation Memories List at the back of the journal.
9. **Pray for anyone who has come to mind .**
10. **Optional: Find a relevant photo and stick it in this journal to remind you.**

INDEX

A

Appreciation
- An appreciation memory 40
- Appreciation memories list 84
- People who invested in you 76
- Places I appreciate 13
- What is special about people you appreciate? 32
- Your favorite food and drink 77
- Your favorite movies, TV shows and comedy clips 76
- Your favorite toys as a child 22

E

Everyday things 37

G

Giving attention to your day with God 74

Gratitude
- Beginning with gratitude 14
- Pets I am grateful for 18
- Photo activities 75
- The good in my life right now 72
- What do I feel grateful for? 15

L

Looking to the future 73

M

Memories
- A calm or happy memory 34
- Engaging with a God memory 28
- Memories to avoid 21

N

Notes pages 78

Noticing and Naming our experiences of God 26

P

Pass it on
- Bringing appreciation of others into your prayer life 66

    Changing relationships by appreciating others 46
    Changing relationships by being appreciative of others 61
    Enriching your family relationships 48
    Remembering together: Life sharing stories 44
    Reminiscing 62
  Planning to be appreciative 36

R

  References 78
  Remember the difference your faith makes 30

S

  Steps 1-7
    Step 1 Get started 12
    Step 2. Remember things you appreciate and are grateful for 16
    Step 3. Relive positive memories 20
    Step 5 Engage with your God-memories 26
    Step 6 Do it through the day 36
    Step 7 Pass it on 42, 54
  Summaries
    Through the day - Review 40
    Using the Daily 1-2-3 Pages 17

T

  Three times a day for 30 days 55

Printed in Great Britain
by Amazon

14175445R00052